THE
CHEYENNE
INDIANS

THE JUNIOR LIBRARY OF
AMERICAN INDIANS

THE CHEYENNE INDIANS

Liz Sonneborn

CHELSEA HOUSE PUBLISHERS
New York   Philadelphia

FRONTISPIECE: Northern Cheyenne leaders Dull Knife and Little Wolf, photographed in the 1870s.

CHAPTER TITLE ORNAMENT: An illustration of a mounted warrior, based on a drawing by a 19th-century Cheyenne artist.

Chelsea House Publishers

EDITOR-IN-CHIEF Remmel Nunn
MANAGING EDITOR Karyn Gullen Browne
COPY CHIEF Mark Rifkin
PICTURE EDITOR Adrian G. Allen
ART DIRECTOR Maria Epes
ASSISTANT ART DIRECTOR Noreen Romano
MANUFACTURING MANAGER Gerald Levine
SYSTEMS MANAGER Lindsey Ottman
PRODUCTION MANAGER Joseph Romano
PRODUCTION COORDINATOR Marie Claire Cebrián

Staff for THE CHEYENNE INDIANS

COPY EDITOR Joseph Roman
EDITORIAL ASSISTANT Michele Haddad
DESIGNER Debora Smith
PICTURE RESEARCHER Diana Gongora
COVER ILLUSTRATOR Vilma Ortiz

First Printing

1 3 5 7 9 8 6 4 2

Library of Congress Cataloging-in-Publication Data

Sonneborn, Liz
   The Cheyenne Indians/by Liz Sonneborn.
      p.   cm.—(The Junior library of American Indians)
   Includes index.
   Summary: Examines the history, culture, and future prospects of the Cheyenne Indians.
   ISBN 0-7910-1654-4
   1. Cheyenne Indians—Juvenile literature. [1. Cheyenne Indians.
2. Indians of North America.] I. Title. II. Series.   91-10577
E99.C53S66 1991   CIP
973'.04973—dc20   AC

CONTENTS

CHAPTER **1**

From Mud and Breath

Long ago, the Creator formed the first human from mud. He then blew his breath into the mud figure, and the person came alive.

After making more people in this way, the Creator set about teaching them how to live. He taught them how to gather and prepare wild foods. He also explained how to use spears to hunt small animals.

The humans lived in a land surrounded by water. There, they often went hungry, so they left to find a new home. In time, they came upon a place rich in larger animals. Encouraged, the people pressed on in search of an even better area in which to settle.

In the course of their travels, two young men went off by themselves for many months. When they returned, they announced that they had found the perfect land for the people. The humans journeyed there and discovered the place was, in fact, full of game. But it was also inhabited by ferocious animals that stood 20 to 30 feet high and ate human beings. The people lived in caves until their population had become so large that the giant animals were afraid to attack them. The human beings then emerged from their caves and moved into an open place. There, their hunting skills improved. At last, they were able to take care of themselves.

This is one version of the Cheyenne Indians' story of their creation. It was written by John Stands in Timber, who became the historian of the tribe in the middle of the 1900s. Throughout his lifetime, Stands in Timber interviewed many older Cheyennes and recorded their stories about the tribe in his book *Cheyenne Memories*. Many of these tales he also remembered from his childhood, when his elders first told him what it meant to be a Cheyenne.

For most of their existence, the Cheyennes did not read about their past in history books. Like John Stands in Timber, they instead listened to the old stories told to them by relatives, usually their grandparents. The grandparents had heard these stories from their own grandparents, who had heard them long ago from theirs.

Today both Indians and non-Indians turn to other sources as well to find out about the Cheyennes. For information about how their ancestors lived very long ago, scientists called archaeologists study objects—such as pottery and tools—that these ancient people left behind. Historians turn to written sources of the past. The Cheyennes had no written language, so these sources do not explain what the Cheyennes did or how they thought. Instead, they offer the impressions that their non-Indian authors had of the Cheyennes' actions and beliefs. Some of the non-Indians who met the Cheyennes in earlier centuries were friendly and welcomed by the tribe. But others were rightly regarded by the Indians as a threat to their well-being.

The first non-Indians to encounter the Cheyennes were Frenchmen who in 1680 were exploring what is now the central United States. Led by René-Robert Cavelier, Sieur de La Salle, this expedition met with many Indian groups during its travels. La Salle and his men came upon the Chey-

Bear Butte, a mountain in South Dakota mentioned in many of the Cheyennes' sacred stories

ennes at Fort Crèvecœur, a post they were building on the Illinois River.

At this time, the Cheyennes inhabited a region to the north, on the banks of the Minnesota River in present-day Minnesota. There, they built farming communities that included many lodges constructed from earth. But this settled way of life was soon going to disappear. Within a matter of decades, the Cheyennes would see great change. This change would lead them to gain the reputation by which they are best known today. They would become the masters of the *Great Plains.* ▲

On horseback, the Cheyennes were able to hunt the herds of buffalo that roamed the Great Plains.

CHAPTER **2**

Masters of the Plains

In the early 1700s, the Cheyennes frequently left their homes to search for a new territory. Usually, these were not moves they wanted to make. Instead, they were pushed out of their lands by larger tribes, such as the Crees, the Ojibwas, the Sioux, and the Assiniboins.

The situation changed, however, in about 1740. The Cheyennes then obtained something that would alter their life forever—the horse. Horses were first introduced to North America by Spanish explorers almost 200 years earlier. Indians in the Southwest acquired these animals from the Spanish and over time began to trade them to Plains tribes, such as the Kiowas and the Comanches. These groups, in turn, traded them to the Cheyennes. Many Cheyenne men were strong, tall, and limber—physical traits that helped them quickly become excellent horsemen.

In fact, the Cheyennes became such good riders that their old enemies could no longer threaten them. Warriors on horseback had a great advantage over warriors on foot. And soon, the Cheyennes were among the most skilled and feared mounted fighters on the Plains.

Instead of merely fending off attacks, Cheyenne war parties began to stage conquests of their own. Aided by their allies the Arapahos and Sioux, they battled the Mandans, the Crows, the Shoshones, the Utes, and the Kiowas. But their greatest enemy was the Pawnees. With this mighty tribe the Cheyennes fought for control of territory in what is now Nebraska and western Kansas. From this area, the Cheyennes could travel south and raid the enormous horse herds of the Comanches. Horse stealing was not considered a crime among the Indians of the Great Plains. Rather, a successful horse thief was respected for his courage and skill.

The Cheyennes and Pawnees fought over these lands for still another reason.

The prairies in this territory were rich with buffalo. These huge animals could provide Plains Indians with virtually every necessity. A buffalo's meat and fat provided a great deal of food. Its hide could be made into leather for clothes and horse gear. The hide could also be used to make a different type of dwelling—a *tipi*. This cone-shaped house was constructed from a frame of wood covered by about 10 to 20 hides stitched together into 1 large piece. The Cheyennes came to prefer tipis to their old earthen houses because tipis were portable. The Indians had to be able to move from place to place in order to follow the roaming herds.

The Cheyennes learned the advantages of hunting on horseback. Previously, individual hunters could only stalk small animals. If they wanted to kill big game, such as a buffalo, they had to assemble a large group of people to chase the animal into an area where it could be trapped and killed. But mounted hunters could chase buffalo themselves. On a properly trained horse, they could ride close enough to their prey to kill it with a single arrow. The best hunters could even time their attack so that their arrow passed through the body of one buffalo and into the hide of a second.

Most hunting and warring was done by men. Young boys were instructed early in the skills they would need to take on these responsibilities. They were taught how to use weapons, especially spears and bows and arrows. But equally important, they learned how to train a horse. A well-trained horse was essential to a Cheyenne hunter and warrior.

A tool, made from a buffalo bone, that was used to scrape animal hides clean

A boy could gain status within the tribe if he proved himself skillful at these activities. One reward for a talented young fighter was admittance into a military society. The Cheyennes had five such groups of warriors: the Fox, the Elk, the Shield, the Dog, and the Bowstring. The members of each society had their own style of dress. They also had special songs and dances that could be performed only by society members. In the 1800s, the Dog society became known as the *Dog Soldiers*. This group included many of the most feared warriors riding the Plains.

The Cheyennes admired their best fighters. But their greatest respect went to their leaders, who were called chiefs by non-Indians. Chiefs usually received their position only after they had distinguished themselves in war. But other qualities were also necessary in a chief. These men had to prove themselves to be calm, generous, kind, sympathetic, and courageous.

At any one time, the Cheyennes were ruled by 44 chiefs. These chiefs held a council whenever a problem arose within the tribe. Issues commonly discussed included whether they should move a hunting camp or whether they should form an alliance with another tribe.

Like hunting and fighting, governing was the domain of Cheyenne men. However, many duties that were just as important fell to the women of the tribe. Women were responsible for gathering and preparing the wild plants that made up much of the Cheyenne diet. They also tanned buffalo hides, sewed clothing, and packed up hunting camps when it was time to move. All the tools they used when performing this work they made themselves.

The respect given women was reflected in the Cheyenne marriage ceremony. When a man wished to marry, he asked an older relative, usually a woman, to visit the woman he wanted to wed. The visitor presented the bride-to-be with gifts and told her about the man's best qualities. After the visitor left, the woman and her family discussed the potential groom's proposal. The next day, they announced whether they had decided to accept or reject it.

If the marriage was approved, the bride, wearing a buckskin dress, mounted the finest horse her family owned. The horse was then led to the house of the groom by an old woman. Custom held that this woman could not be related to the bride. The groom's relatives lifted the bride off the horse, set her down upon a special blanket, and carried her into the house. There, the groom's female relatives gave her new clothing, dressed her hair, and painted her face. The ceremony concluded with a great feast, and both families showered the couple with gifts.

A marriage ceremony was not the only ritual observed by the Cheyennes. One of the most sacred was the Renewal of the Medicine Arrows. On the longest day of the year, the entire tribe gathered for the ceremony in a large open area near a stream. There, they all set up their tipis in a wide circle. Within the circle, they erected a special structure—the Keeper of the Arrows. In the circle's exact center, they built a huge tipi that was called the Sacred Arrow Lodge. Inside it, religious leaders opened a leather bundle that held a bunch of arrows. The Cheyennes believed that two of these arrows could render a buffalo powerless. Two others could do the same thing to human enemies.

Another important Cheyenne ritual—the Sun Dance—was performed by other Plains Indians as well. During the Sun Dance, young men proved their courage by threading a leather thong through two holes punctured in their chest. They then stood for hours in front of a pole to which the end of

the thong was tied. The rite was very pain-
ful, allowing a man to display to his fellow
tribespeople his ability to withstand great
hardship.

The Cheyennes' religious ceremonies,
political structure, and values all contributed
to one goal—to keep them strong. The
tribe's strength allowed them to become

Cheyenne men
preparing to perform
the Sun Dance

leaders on the Plains. As such, they were able to choose which other Indian groups they wanted as their allies and which they wanted as their enemies. In the coming years, more and more non-Indians would arrive in their lands, presenting the Cheyennes with a new challenge: deciding whether these strangers were to be their friends or their foes. ◬

CHAPTER **3**

Meeting Strangers

In 1803, on behalf of the newly formed United States, President Thomas Jefferson bought a huge tract of land from France. This area, known as the Louisiana Purchase, stretched from the Mississippi River to the Rocky Mountains. Both countries believed that France owned this land. Even though Indians had inhabited the region for hundreds of years, neither nation thought the Indian groups who lived there had any claim to their own homelands.

At the time of the purchase, Jefferson did not know exactly what he had bought. Past explorers had traveled through only a small part of the vast expanse of territory. In 1804, the president chose two men, Meriwether Lewis and William Clark, to lead an expedition to find out more about the region. They were to bring back information about the terrain, the plants, the animals, and most of all, the people they encountered.

Among the many Indians Lewis and Clark met were a group of Cheyennes who were visiting a Mandan village. As a gesture of friendship, Clark offered one Cheyenne chief a small medal. Instead of being pleased, the chief drew back in alarm. He explained that he knew that white people were "medicine" and that he feared that objects they carried could do him harm.

The chief's reaction probably stemmed from an incident that had happened about 10 years before. A French trader had given a Cheyenne leader called the Lance several gifts in exchange for a promise to be kind to strangers in his lands. The Lance later broke his vow by murdering a family of Sioux living among the Cheyennes. Soon after the crime, three of the Lance's children died, and lightning struck his brother's dwelling. Some Cheyennes took these events as a sign that white people's presence among them was a bad omen.

In the early 1800s, few white visitors bore out the Cheyennes' worst fears. In fact, most of them actively sought the Indians' friendship. Some of the whites journeyed to the Indians' camps in order to trade goods with them. But others who arrived in the Plains were looking only for adventure. The journals of these traders and adventurers are the best written records of how the Cheyennes lived before they had had much contact with non-Indians.

Only two years after Lewis and Clark's expedition, two Canadian traders, Charles MacKenzie and Alexander Henry, had a very different encounter with the Cheyennes. These men were friendly with the Mandans and the Hidatsas, who asked the traders to come with them to a meeting with the Cheyennes. The two groups of Indians wanted to become the Cheyennes' trading partners but were wary of the tribe. The skill of Cheyenne warriors was well known to them.

After traveling for six days, the members of the trading party came upon the Cheyennes. They saw before them nearly 100 horses, each mounted by a warrior carrying a shield and a lance. The animals themselves wore frightening masks that resembled the heads of wild beasts. Behind the wall of horses and riders were even more Cheyenne warriors on foot.

For a moment, the two groups faced each other in silence. Finally, a Hidatsa chief rode forward and, as a sign of friendship, extended an American flag Lewis and Clark had given him years before. The Hidatsas, the Mandans, and the two traders breathed a sigh of relief when one Cheyenne took the banner and hugged its Hidatsa bearer.

The trading sessions among the Indians went well until a group of Assiniboin Indians joined their camp. The Mandans and Hidatsas were on good terms with the Assiniboins. The Cheyennes, however, well remembered that in years past the Assiniboins had destroyed some of their villages. Angry about the presence of their enemies, the Cheyenne traders grew sullen and uncooperative. Alarmed by their change in attitude, the Mandans and Hidatsas left the camp earlier than they had originally planned.

MacKenzie and Henry's report of this incident reveals the powerful position of the Cheyennes at this time. Other Indian groups respected them and sought their friendship. But these tribes also feared the Cheyennes, knowing only too well what might happen if the Cheyenne warriors came to see their tribespeople as their enemies.

In 1825, the Cheyennes were again visited by representatives of the U.S. government. But, unlike Lewis and Clark, these

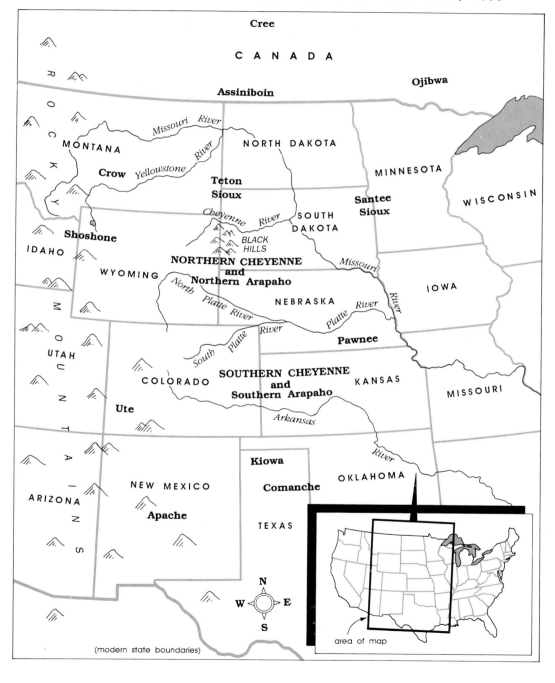

Cree

CANADA

Ojibwa

Assiniboin

Missouri River

MONTANA

NORTH DAKOTA

MINNESOTA

Crow *Yellowstone River*

WISCONSIN

Teton
Sioux

Santee
Sioux

Cheyenne River

SOUTH
DAKOTA

Shoshone

BLACK
HILLS

IDAHO

NORTHERN CHEYENNE
and
Northern Arapaho

Missouri

WYOMING

North Platte River

NEBRASKA

Platte River

River

IOWA

South Platte River

Pawnee

UTAH

COLORADO

SOUTHERN CHEYENNE
and
Southern Arapaho

KANSAS

MISSOURI

Ute

Arkansas

River

Kiowa

OKLAHOMA

NEW MEXICO

Comanche

ARIZONA

Apache

TEXAS

N
W E
S

area of map

(modern state boundaries)

people were sent to do more than get to know the Indians and their land. Led by General Henry Atkinson, the nearly 500 U.S. soldiers came to negotiate a formal peace with the mighty Cheyennes and their neighbors. High-Backed Wolf and several other Cheyenne chiefs met with Atkinson and assured the general that they would like to remain on good terms with the United States. The leaders then signed an agreement, or *treaty*, in which they pledged their friendship.

At the time of Atkinson's visit, the Cheyennes spent most of the year along the Cheyenne River near the Black Hills of present-day South Dakota and Wyoming. However, many tribespeople sometimes journeyed south to the southern edge of the Rocky Mountains in what is now Colorado. Some merely went there in the winter, attracted by the warmer climate. Others wanted to raid the settlements of southern tribes for horses or to hunt the beavers and bears in the region. Over time, a large number of Cheyennes began to settle there permanently, breaking the tribe into two groups, the Southern Cheyennes and the Northern Cheyennes.

In 1828, the Cheyennes were given a new reason to spend time in the south. That year, two brothers, Charles and William

*Trader George Bent
and his Cheyenne
wife, Magpie*

Bent, met a party of Cheyenne horse raiders led by a chief named Yellow Wolf. The Bents were traders and told Yellow Wolf that they would like to deal with his people on a regular basis. The chief suggested that they set up a post downriver.

The post, called Bent's Fort, was visited not only by the Cheyennes but also by non-Indians traveling through the area. American settlers from the east, Mexican settlers from the southeast, and American and French traders arrived there frequently. Many met the Cheyennes and offered them new and unfamiliar goods. A few even spent some time living among the tribe.

The Cheyennes' dealings with these non-Indians were generally friendly. However, they remained at odds with nearby tribes. The Northern Cheyennes fought with the Crows, and the Southern Cheyennes battled the Comanches, the Pawnees, and the Kiowas. Often, violence erupted because the Cheyennes stole horses from another group's herds. On one such raid, a party of Cheyennes was discovered and murdered by Kiowa and Comanche warriors before they could escape.

Chief Yellow Wolf was determined to avenge the deaths. In 1838, he led a force of Cheyenne and Arapaho fighters in an attack on a Kiowa-Comanche camp. During the conflict—later named the Battle of Wolf Creek—the Cheyennes and the Arapahos killed nearly 50 members of the enemy tribes.

By this time, many more American settlers were journeying to the area around Bent's Fort. The U.S. government became afraid that it could not protect these citizens if the fighting among the Indians continued.

A sketch of Yellow Wolf made by a U.S. Army lieutenant in 1845

To end the violence, American officials called a peace council at the fort and invited the warring groups. The tribes all agreed to a pact of friendship.

The council marked the beginning of U.S. officials' interference in the dealings these Indians had with one another. At the same time, the goods and customs brought to the Cheyennes by traveling non-Indians began to affect the Indians' way of life. One important example was alcohol. The Cheyennes had never tasted whiskey before it was given to them by non-Indians. Some traders took advantage of the Indians by getting them drunk on the brew and swindling them. In his 1856 autobiography, trader Jim Beckwourth explained that he tricked Cheyenne chiefs Bob-tailed Horse and Old Bark by giving them both a pint of whiskey worth about six cents each. In exchange, he received 2 buffalo robes, which Beckwourth could sell for $10.

But most non-Indian guests in Cheyenne camps at this time dealt with the Indians fairly and were impressed by their hosts. George Ruxton, an Englishman who visited a Cheyenne village near Bent's Fort in 1845, remembered it as a "Pretty Encampment." He was especially struck by the tipis of the warriors and chiefs. These homes were decorated with paintings that told stories of their inhabitants' heroic deeds.

Another visitor, Lewis Garrard from Cincinnati, Ohio, spent two months among the Cheyennes along the Arkansas River during the winter of 1846–47. The young adventurer was fascinated by Cheyenne camp life. He noted that the Indians loved playing games and gambling, marveled at the beautiful brass rings and bracelets worn by Cheyenne women, and admired a Cheyenne man's tenderness as he held his young son and sang to him. Garrard also learned of the Cheyennes' effective method of punishing an unruly child. A parent would pour icy water over the youngster's head until the boy or girl calmed down.

By the middle of the 1800s, the Cheyennes were accustomed to dealing with non-Indians. And non-Indians were well aware of the Cheyennes' power in the regions where they lived. The Northern Cheyennes now stayed west of the Black Hills, the Southern Cheyennes remained near Bent's Fort, and another group lived in between, along the South Platte River. But they were still all Cheyennes, sharing traditions and customs that the many recent newcomers to their lands had come to respect. ▲

*Cheyenne leaders
White Antelope,
Alights-on-the-Cloud,
and Roman Nose*

CHAPTER 4

Promises of Peace

By the mid-1800s, the U.S. government decided that the fighting among Indian groups and among Indians and settlers on the Plains had to stop. More and more Americans from the East were traveling through the area. Some wanted to find a place to settle and build farms or ranches. Others hoped to become rich by mining gold in California and in other western regions where the mineral had been discovered. The U.S. Army built forts along the trails the Americans traveled. But it was clear that these posts were not enough to keep clashes from occurring.

To establish peace in the Plains, U.S. officials organized one of the biggest treaty

35

councils ever. In 1851, Indians from all the major Plains tribes were asked to come to Fort Laramie in what is now southeastern Colorado. Soon, hundreds of warriors arrived on horseback, and the tipis of 10,000 Indians surrounded the fort.

The council was a colorful and entertaining spectacle. The tribes took turns hosting fabulous feasts for one another. During one such celebration, a group of Cheyennes demonstrated their excellent horsemanship and fighting skills. They ended the display with a war dance, during which they recounted the heroic deeds they had performed in battle.

The main goal of the council was to establish specific boundaries for Indian territories. Wan-es-sah-ta, or He Who Walks with His Toes Turned Out, was chosen to speak to the Americans on behalf of the Cheyennes. The treaty that resulted established four borders for Cheyenne-Arapaho territory: the North Platte River in the north, the Arkansas River in the south, a line through western Kansas in the east, and the Rocky Mountains in the west.

To the government's disappointment, the Treaty of Fort Laramie did not create harmony on the Plains. Too many whites were moving west too quickly. In 1853 alone,

15,000 non-Indians passed through Fort Laramie. These travelers often abused Indians and hunted in their lands. Even worse, they brought European diseases, such as smallpox and measles, that the Indians had never had before. The germs spread quickly, causing Indians to become ill and die in large numbers.

As tensions increased, so did outbreaks of violence. Both settlers and Indians attacked each other. And after an attack, the victims often retaliated, making the fighting go on and on. For example, in 1856 in Laramie, Wyoming, an army officer arrested three Cheyenne men and then shot one. The Cheyennes were outraged. Seeking revenge, they staged a series of assaults on settlers, including one on the driver of a mail wagon traveling to Fort Kearny in Nebraska. Army troops responded by killing 10 Cheyennes in camps surrounding the fort. This action led Cheyenne warriors to attack still more settlements.

In the summer of 1857, the army decided a larger-scale assault on the Cheyennes was in order. It chose Colonel E. V. Sumner to lead the operation. Sumner had gained the nickname Bull of the Woods because he was such a ferocious fighter. His troops battled a force of Cheyennes on the

Republican River and killed between 20 and 30 men. This conflict was the first major confrontation between the Cheyennes and the U.S. Army. But it would not be the last.

At this time, the Cheyennes had other problems in addition to the continual fighting. Disease was still killing many people. Settlers were taking control of the best land in their territory. And the traffic of travelers was disrupting the movement of buffalo herds, making hunting nearly impossible.

In 1859, the Northern Cheyennes decided to sell a large amount of land to the U.S. government. In exchange, they were given a *reservation* along the Laramie River in southeastern Wyoming. A reservation was a tract of land that was set aside only for Indians. The government guaranteed that settlers would never be allowed to invade its boundaries. The Northern Cheyennes were also to receive an annuity, or yearly payment, of $16,000. Their leaders felt that this sum would help their ill and hungry people.

The next year, the Southern Cheyennes and the Arapahos also agreed to settle on a reservation. Chiefs Black Kettle, White Antelope, Lean Bear, Little Wolf, Tall Bear, and Left Hand signed a treaty in which they promised to move to a tract just north of the

A rawhide rattle shaken during Cheyenne war dances

Arkansas River. The government, in turn, said it would provide the Indians with food, clothing, and other goods.

Soon, the Southern Cheyennes became discontented with their new home. The land was so dry it was unfit for farming or hunting. In addition, the government did not give them the necessities as it had promised. In September 1861, the angry Cheyennes gathered at Fort Wise, a post near Bent's Fort. They demanded that the fort commander provide them with food and goods. He claimed he had few supplies himself but gave the Indians enough goods to prevent violence from erupting.

Tensions on the Plains continued to mount. In 1863, a group of chiefs were called to Washington, D.C., to discuss with the president ways to maintain peace. The Cheyennes sent Lean Bear, War Bonnet, and Standing in the Water to represent them.

Lean Bear spoke for the group in a meeting with President Abraham Lincoln. The chief explained that he wanted peace but that whites seemed to prefer war. Lincoln assured him that he, too, wanted the violence to end. The president added that he would make every to effort to see that whites would not break the promises stated in past treaties.

Satisfied, Lean Bear left Washington. But the fighting went on. Two army officers—Colonel John M. Chivington and Lieutenant George S. Eayre—were particularly eager to punish the Cheyennes for their continued raids on white settlements.

continued on page 49

FROM THE BUFFALO

The Cheyennes obtained almost everything they needed from the buffalo they hunted. The animal's hide was especially useful. The material was sewn into tipi covers, clothing, shoes, and storage containers. Hide was also used to make beautiful paintings that celebrated the Cheyennes' greatest hunters and warriors.

This painting captures the essence of the Cheyenne horseman—a superb rider and marksman, adept with gun and bow.

Cheyenne women were remarkably resourceful, incorporating a wide array of objects—including animal teeth and bones—into their handiwork. When white traders arrived, they brought new materials, such as metal, beads, and cloth, that soon found their way onto Cheyenne designs.

A saddle blanket (opposite) from the 1840s made of buffalo hide and decorated with beads and cloth.

In a pipe bag (above right), horsehair and feathers, standard Cheyenne decorations, are fitted with metal pieces obtained from traders.

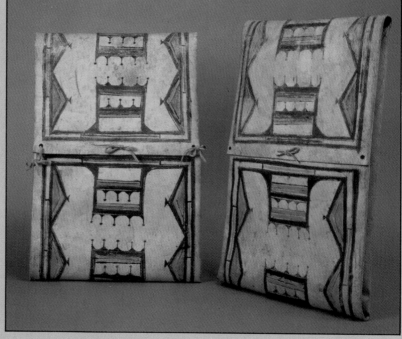

ass tacks form crosses on 's cradleboard (above).

These parfleches, or storage cases, date from the 1880s. They are made of rawhide decorated with store-bought paint.

The Cheyennes excelled not only as craft workers but also as painters. For canvases they used the skin of deer, elk, and buffalo, which they covered with bold hues. Horses—usually shown in the heat of battle or during the hunt—are depicted with uncommon grace.

This hide shows mounted Cheyennes raiding a herd of wild horses.

Cheyenne horsemen battle the U.S. Cavalry in this hide painting.

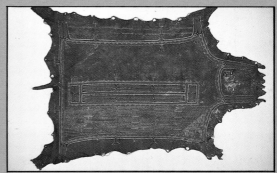

This painting done in 1890 includes materials obtained from whites: a muslin canvas (softer than hide) and commercial paints.

Some buffalo-hide paintings had abstract designs rather than representational figures.

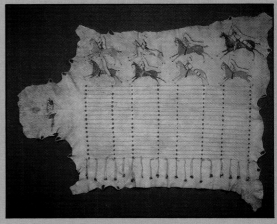

This hide features traditional materials: elk skin, horsehair, and deer toes.

The painstaking job of making clothes fell to Cheyenne women. Their main material was animal hide, which they prepared with four tools: a scraper, for cleaning the hide of meat and fat; a flesher, for thinning the hide; a draw blade, for shaving off hair; and a rope, for softening the skin into workable material. This process took several days and produced the men's garments shown here.

A beaded vest, made in the 1890s, features warriors and eagles, whose feathers were prized by the Cheyennes.

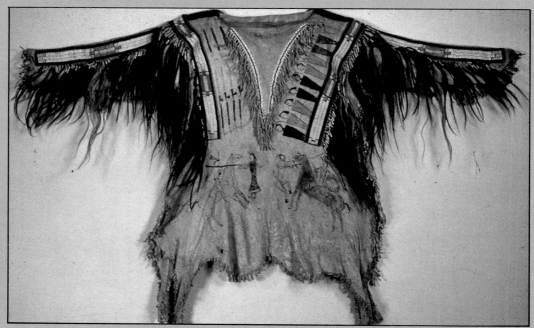

This shirt is decorated with porcupine-quill embroidery.

The fringed flaps on these high winter boots are made of deerskin. Cheyenne women often worked beads into geometric patterns. Here the blend of colors is superb.

The most common form of Cheyenne
footwear was the moccasin, made of a
single piece of hide folded over, with a
second hide sewn on to form a thick
sole. Shoes were decorated with beads
and quills.

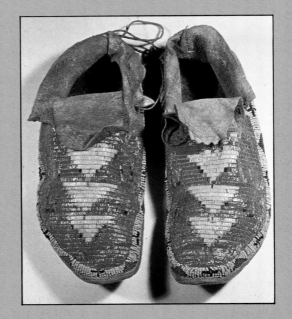

Right: *A Northern Cheyenne woman
made the patterns on these moccasins
with dyed quills.*

These moccasins were used in the
Ghost Dance ceremony.

continued from page 40

On May 16, 1864, Eayre's troops encountered a large group of Cheyennes hunting buffalo north of Fort Larned. The hunt was led by Lean Bear, who had just got back from his trip. The chief and another Indian rode forward to greet the troops. On his chest, he wore a medal that Lincoln had given him. In his hand, he held a note from the president that said the chief could be trusted. As the two got close to the line of soldiers, the troops opened fired and then retreated to the fort. Both Lean Bear and his companion were killed.

The incident pushed the Cheyennes over the brink. The Dog Soldiers were particularly angered. They struck wagon trains and settlements with a new fury.

It looked as though a full-scale war was likely. Lieutenant Eayre ordered all Indians who wanted to remain friends with the United States to report to various forts. There, he implied, they would be safe from the soldiers' bullets.

Black Kettle and other Cheyenne leaders were hesitant to follow Eayre's orders. But Major Edward W. Wynkoop, an officer who was sympathetic to the Cheyennes, convinced them to trust the army. In November, a small group of Cheyennes arrived at Fort Lyon. They reported that 600 others were on their way and 2,000 more would eventually follow.

However, hundreds of Arapahos had already reached the fort. There was little food for them, and some were starving. The commander of the fort told the Cheyennes, led by Black Kettle, to go back to their camp at the bend of Sand Creek, just north of the fort. The officer said they would be safe there.

Meanwhile, Chivington ordered a regiment of volunteers to march to Sand Creek. This regiment, the Colorado Third, was known within the army as the Bloodless Third. The nickname was meant to be an insult. The group had never fought in a battle, had never spilled any blood. The young volunteers were all eager to fight. If they

A drawing of the Sand Creek Massacre

could prove themselves in war, maybe they could lose their shameful nickname once and for all.

At dawn, the 700 soldiers on horseback reached Sand Creek and spied the Indian camp. All was quiet until a few camp dogs barked. Sure they had been discovered by the Indians, Chivington ordered his troops to charge the rows of tipis. The noise awakened the Cheyennes, who stepped outside into a rain of bullets. The men fought to fend off the soldiers, while the women and children rushed to the bed of the creek, searching for a place to hide. They were discovered by the volunteers and slaughtered. Chief White Antelope approached his attackers with his hands held high, begging them not to shoot. He was also struck down. Black Kettle raised an American flag to show the troops that his people were friends with the United States. His message was ignored, and the chief barely escaped with his life.

When the *massacre* was over, between 400 and 500 Indian corpses covered the ground where the camp had been. The United States had pledged to make peace with the Cheyennes. Now the Cheyennes felt they knew just how much they could trust the government's promises. ⌃

U.S. troops on an
1874 expedition to
the Black Hills

CHAPTER **5**

The Last Stand

News of the Sand Creek Massacre spread quickly. The Southern Cheyennes were shocked and infuriated by Chivington's betrayal. At a meeting of nearly 2,000 Cheyenne, Arapaho, and Sioux fighters, war leaders declared that the time for a war against the whites was at hand.

Americans were divided in their opinion of what to do next. Frightened settlers in the West urged a military campaign. Many officials in Washington, D.C., though, still hoped for a peaceful solution. Peace councils were called in 1865 and again in 1867. At both, Cheyenne chiefs signed new treaties.

But the Indian leaders had little confidence in the United States's peacemaking efforts. At the 1865 council, Black Kettle opened the talks with a moving speech: "I once thought that I was the only man that persevered to be the friend of the white man, but since they have come and (robbed) our lodges, horses and everything else, it is hard for me to believe white men any more."

The treaties did little to quell the rage of most Cheyennes. Raids on white settlements continued, especially in Kansas. Settlers demands for protection by soldiers also grew louder.

General Philip H. Sheridan, the commander of the army in Kansas, decided to take action. He set up a special unit of 50 soldiers led by Colonel George A. Forsyth. Sheridan reasoned that a small force could move quickly and therefore ferret out Indian raiders more easily than a larger group of soldiers could.

But Sheridan was wrong. Forsyth's soldiers were quashed in an unexpected Cheyenne attack. Leading one charge was the great Cheyenne warrior known as Roman Nose. As he fought, he wore a magnificent headdress decorated with so many feathers it trailed behind him.

After the defeat, Sheridan developed a new strategy. Instead of battling on the open prairie, his soldiers would attack the Cheyennes in their home camps during the winter. The Indians got wind of the general's plan and set up many of their camps farther south than they usually did. But few chiefs thought the U.S. Army would attack in the winter. They believed that the soldiers were too weak to be able to stand the cold.

In late 1868, Sheridan sent out three forces of soldiers. By mid-November, the main group reached the junction of Beaver and Wolf creeks, in what is now northwestern Oklahoma. There, they erected Camp Supply.

One regiment, the Seventh Cavalry commanded by Lieutenant General George Custer, left the camp and marched along Wolf Creek. Soon, they found an Indian trail that traced a snow-covered prairie leading to the Washita River. In a bend in the river, they found what they were looking for—an encampment of Cheyennes.

At dawn on November 27, 1864, Custer and his men attacked. Soldiers killed men, women, and children just as they had at Sand Creek. In fact, the Cheyennes they murdered were the survivors of the earlier massacre. Among the dead was the great peacemaker Black Kettle.

Cheyennes in encampments downriver heard of the killings and rushed to confront

General George Custer

the Seventh Cavalry. Before they could stage a counterattack, Custer's men managed to escape and retreat safely to Camp Supply. But the Cheyennes and Custer would meet again.

Meanwhile, the fighting went on. One of the conflicts most devastating to the Cheyennes occurred in July 1869. Earlier, Tall Bull's band of Dog Soldiers launched a series of raids on settlements and outposts of the Kansas Pacific Railroad, taking prisoners during each. In revenge for these attacks, troops commanded by Major E. A. Carr stormed the warriors' village located north of the Platte River. In a daylong battle, Carr's forces killed 52 Cheyennes, including Tall Bull. The defeat marked the end of the Cheyennes' occupation of the area between the Platte and the Arkansas. Even worse, the battle caused the mighty Dog Soldiers to disband.

The continual fighting had taken its toll on the Southern Cheyennes. Many were so beaten down that they voluntarily traveled to Camp Supply. Putting themselves at the mercy of the U.S. government, they asked for food and shelter from the *Quakers* living there. These people were members of a religious group, the Society of Friends, that opposed war. President Ulysses S. Grant had asked them to help the impoverished Indians of the West.

The Cheyennes also met Quakers at Darlington Agency. This compound was the center of a reservation, in what is now central Oklahoma, that President Grant had given to the Cheyennes and the Arapahos.

There, a Quaker named Brinton Darlington was the *agent*—a government official charged with dealing with Indians in a specific area. Although in his sixties, Darlington had the enthusiasm of a young man. At the agency, he busily built a sawmill, cleared cornfields, and erected a school for Indian children.

Like other sympathetic whites, Darlington believed that if the Indians learned to live like their American neighbors, the fighting would stop. But he did not understand that the Cheyennes wanted to keep their old ways. They loved riding through the Plains and craved the excitement of the buffalo hunt. Few were interested in performing the difficult, often boring labor of a settled farmer. The army also did not like the Quakers' plan. They wanted to see the Indians removed from the Plains, not living peacefully side by side with whites.

Most Southern Cheyennes steered clear of camps and agencies. They preferred to live in their traditional encampments, even if they were starving and ill. But these peoples' morale grew worse when they learned that a party of whites had come to Kansas to measure land there. The Cheyennes knew that these surveyors had been sent to prepare for the building of a railroad.

· CHEYENNE COUNRTY IN THE LATE 1800s ·

MONTANA

Little
Bighorn
1876

Yellowstone River

Missouri River

Tongue River

Powder River

Bighorn River

Rosebud
1876

NORTH DAKOTA

MINNESOTA

SOUTH DAKOTA

River

WYOMING

North Platte

Cheyenne

Wounded Knee
1890

Pine Ridge Agency
Red Cloud Agency

Fort
Robinson

Missouri

IOWA

Fort Laramie

River

NEBRASKA

Platte River

River

Fort Kearny

River

UTAH

South Platte River

COLORADO

Sand
Creek
1864

KANSAS

Fort Larned

MISSOURI

Bent's Fort

Arkansas

River

Camp
Supply

NEW MEXICO

Washita
1868

Fort
Reno

Darlington
Agency

OKLAHOMA

TEXAS

Red

River

area of map

0   100   200   300 miles

△   Indian agencies

✕   Battle sites

◤   Forts/trading posts

(modern state boundaries)

N
W — E
S

They also knew that trains would bring more and more whites into their lands.

In the spring of 1873, a group of Cheyennes murdered the entire surveying party. The action sparked another string of raids in which more settlers and surveyors were killed. In the latest round of violence, Sheridan saw an opportunity. The Indians' attacks, he claimed, proved that the Quakers' peace plan had failed. Sheridan announced that it was now clear that the only way to deal with the Cheyennes was his way—by force.

Throughout 1874, men under his command harassed the Southern Cheyennes, burning their tipis and stealing their horses and supplies. Few Indians were killed, but many came to feel that there was no place to hide from the army. By the end of the year, many Cheyennes had surrendered.

Among the last to do so was a group of 821 people who arrived at Camp Supply in March 1875. Most turned in their weapons to the post authorities. But several Indians secretly kept their guns.

When the troops tried to place iron cuffs around the ankles of some of the Cheyenne warriors, an argument broke out. A young man named Black Horse objected and then tried to escape from the camp. The soldiers gunned him down. The Cheyennes who still had their guns shot back and fled. Most were rounded up by troops. The war leaders among them were packed in a railway car and sent off to Fort Marion, a prison in Florida. The event marked the end of the Southern Cheyennes' resistance to the U.S. Army.

The Northern Cheyennes, however, had not given up the fight. They made known their determination to stay on their lands. In 1873, the U.S. government had tried to move the Northern Cheyennes to a reservation in present-day Oklahoma occupied by their southern kin. But the Northern Cheyennes refused. Their chiefs explained to President Grant that they would rather die than leave their homeland.

The government agreed to the group's demands at that time. But only two years later, the U.S. officials began to rethink their position. Gold had been discovered in the Black Hills, an area long frequented by Cheyenne, Arapaho, and Sioux Indians. The United States wanted this valuable land and asked to buy it from the tribes. The Indians told them no. In the spring of 1876, the government decided to send in the army to force them out.

In early June, a large force commanded by General George Crook reached the head of the Rosebud Creek in southeastern Montana. There, the soldiers attacked a group of Northern Cheyennes and Sioux. The conflict ended when Crook's men turned back to regroup, and the Indians retreated to their camps on the Little Bighorn River. Neither side had clearly won the battle.

Meanwhile, another force, led by General Alfred Terry, approached the region from the west. At the mouth of the Rosebud, the general ordered the Seventh Cavalry, still headed by Custer, to march down an Indian trail. The trail followed the Rosebud Creek and then snaked westward toward the Little Bighorn River valley. There, Custer saw smoke rising from the Indians' camp.

Terry had told Custer to wait for him and his soldiers. But Custer decided to fight the Indians then and there. He divided his troops into three groups. One, led by Captain Frederick Benteen, was to stay behind and scout the area. Another, commanded by Major Marcus Reno, would attack the camp from one side. The third, led by Cus-

A drawing of the Battle of Little Bighorn by Sioux artist Amos Bad Heart Buffalo

ter, would support Reno's men by assault-
ing the other side.

Custer's plan had one enormous flaw—
there were many more Indians in the camp
than he had thought. Immediately after his
men struck, Major Reno saw that the troops

were greatly outnumbered. He had no choice but to retreat.

Reno met up with Benteen, and their combined forces tried to reach Custer to aid his men. But they were halted by a barrage of bullets from the Indians' rifles. Not knowing of Reno's retreat, Custer's troops rode into disaster alone.

The Battle of Little Bighorn lasted probably no longer than an hour. In the end, the bodies of cavalrymen covered the bloody battlefield. Americans everywhere were shocked by newspaper accounts of the carnage witnessed at the scene of what became known as Custer's Last Stand.

The battle was, in a sense, the last stand of the Northern Cheyennes as well. Never again would they see such a victory. After the battle, fearing retaliation, the Cheyennes retreated deep into the hills. Expeditions of soldiers, filled with fury, followed. Despite the Indians' fierce resistance, many were killed. The survivors suffered a terrible winter. By the spring of 1877, most felt they could fight no more and turned themselves over to U.S. authorities.

Later that year, about 1,000 Northern Cheyennes were compelled to join the Southern Cheyennes at Darlington Agency.

Under the blazing sun, they traveled on foot for 70 days. During the grueling trek, two-thirds of the people in the group died of disease. Those who lived thought of little else but when they would see their beautiful northern home again. ⌃

Northern Cheyenne construction workers, photographed in the early 1980s

CHAPTER **6**

A New World

Reservation life proved difficult for both the Southern and the Northern Cheyennes in present-day Oklahoma. But the people of the southern branch at least were living in the region of their birth. For the Northern Cheyennes, the region was unfamiliar and disappointing. They did not like the humid flatlands of the reservation. Remembering the high, dry country of the north, they longed to go home.

Some Northern Cheyennes grew so unhappy that they decided to escape from the reservation. One group of more than 300 people sneaked away the night of September 7, 1878. When the reservation authorities found they were missing, troops were sent out to pursue them.

The chase continued far into the north country. In Nebraska, the escapees who had been able to avoid the soldiers' bullets split into two groups. One surrendered to troops in Wyoming and Montana. The other yielded their weapons to soldiers near Fort Robinson in Nebraska.

Those who surrendered at Fort Robinson were greatly abused. They were locked in an unheated prison in the middle of winter for seven days. During that time, the prisoners were given no food or water. Many starved. Others froze to death. In desperation, the survivors finally leapt from the building's high windows and dashed toward the surrounding hills. Some were shot down, and many were recaptured nearby. A few of the prisoners got away, however. They were never heard from again.

The Cheyennes who remained on the southern reservation did not fare well during the last years of the 1800s. Confined to the reservation boundaries, they had to abandon the buffalo hunt. But even if they had been allowed to travel the Plains, there were no more buffalo left to kill. The great herds of these animals had been slaughtered by white hunters, sometimes just for sport, in only a few decades.

The Indians were left with no choice but to rely on the government to give them food and supplies. Agents, however, did not always provide the Cheyennes with the goods that past treaties promised them. Sometimes, these officials withheld food to make the Cheyennes do whatever they wished.

Different agents had different schemes for how the Indians should make their livelihood now that the buffalo were gone. Some thought the Cheyennes should be

The layout of the Cheyenne-Arapaho Agency in present-day Oklahoma

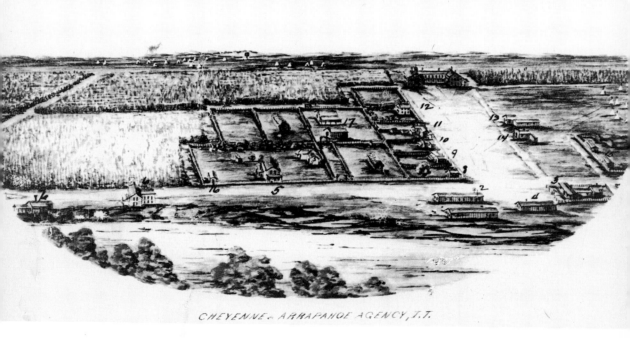

CHEYENNE & ARRAPAHOE AGENCY, I.T.

farmers, but generally the Indians hated and refused to do farm work. The Cheyennes were more receptive to agents who believed they should become cattlemen.

Just as the Cheyennes were finally getting used to the reservation, the government dealt them another blow. In 1887, the United States decided that reservation land should be divided into small tracts, called *allotments*. Each allotment would be owned by an individual. The idea seemed very strange to the Cheyennes. Like other Indian groups, they were accustomed to holding their land in common. No individual Cheyenne owned any one portion of the tribe's land. Instead, all Cheyennes shared their tribal land.

After the government had given an allotment to all the reservation Cheyennes it deemed eligible to get one, there was a large amount of land left over. The United States wanted to buy this surplus and then sell it to whites. The Cheyennes were shocked. The reservation was supposed to have been theirs for all time. Chief Old Crow spoke the feelings of many of his people when he told U.S. officials: "The Great Spirit gave the Indians all this country and never tell them that they should sell it. . . . I don't want money; money doesn't do an Indian any good."

But the government would not let the matter rest. It so pressured the Cheyenne chiefs that they finally gave in to its demands. But still most of the Cheyenne people were miserable that whites were moving onto their land.

Their unhappiness led many to join a new Indian religion: the *Ghost Dance*. Its founder, a medicine man named Wovoka of the Paiute tribe, claimed that he had spoken to Christ, who told him that within two years whites would disappear from the Plains.

A group of Cheyennes preparing for a Ghost Dance ceremony

Wovoka also predicted that the great buffalo herds would return. Indians from many tribes embraced Wovoka's teachings. But when neither of his predictions came true, interest in the Ghost Dance gradually waned.

Not surprisingly, the Cheyennes' agents did not like the Ghost Dance. They disapproved of other customs and rituals that the Cheyennes cherished as well. In the 1890s, Agent A. E. Woodson, a former army officer, outlawed such sacred Cheyenne ceremonies as the Sun Dance and the Medicine Arrow rites. Old Crow and other chiefs resisted Woodson. They clung to their traditional ways. But now, surrounded by whites, non-Indian ways began to creep into Cheyenne society. By the end of the 1800s, many Cheyennes wore non-Indian clothing, lived in non-Indian–style homes, and farmed like their non-Indian neighbors did.

The Cheyennes in the north had similar experiences during this period. They were given a small reservation on the Tongue River in Montana in 1884. Even though the number of animals was quickly dwindling, these Cheyennes were able to survive by eating wild berries and fruits. Over time, they took up farming to increase their food supply just as their ancestors had done long ago.

The Northern Cheyennes also made money by selling hay and firewood to nearby white ranchers. They took up horse breeding as well. The Indians were so successful at this enterprise that the government gave them a number of cows and bulls. The government's guess that the tribespeople would be just as capable with cattle as with horses proved correct.

U.S. officials, however, would not leave well enough alone. In 1919, they decided that the Cheyennes' many horses were destroying the grasslands on which their cattle grazed. Representatives of the government came to the reservation and sold or shot most of the Indians' horses. The number of horses owned by the Northern Cheyennes was reduced from 15,000 to 3,000 in a few years.

The Indians' land was being taken away as well. In the 1920s, the government decided to divide the Northern Cheyennes' reservation into allotments. Like their southern relatives, the Indians lost much of their land to non-Indians in the process.

In the late 1900s, both the Northern and the Southern Cheyennes have suffered

many setbacks. As a result, most of the Southern Cheyennes still live in poverty, although they are increasingly fighting for the chance to receive better educations and well-paying jobs. The Northern Cheyennes have been luckier. In the 1960s, coal was discovered on their land. This valuable mineral gave them a new source of income, but it brought them problems, too. Some unscrupulous businesspeople tricked the Indians out of much of their coal sales money. The Northern Cheyennes also discovered that the companies that were to extract the coal planned to strip-mine their land. Strip mining destroys the environment. Only by enlisting the help of a lawyer were the Cheyennes able to save their land.

Both branches of the Cheyenne Indians now inhabit two worlds. In many ways, they live just like non-Indian Americans. They drive automobiles, eat hamburgers, go to movies, enjoy popular music—do everything that their white neighbors do. But in some ways, the Cheyennes are unique. They still know and treasure the ancient ceremonies, customs, and history of their tribe. Although many things have been lost to them over time, their pride in being Cheyenne Indians remains as alive as ever. ▲

Northern Cheyennes performing a traditional dance in the early 1980s

CHRONOLOGY

1680   French explorer René-Robert Cavelier, Sieur de
            La Salle, meets a group of Cheyennes along the
            Illinois River

ca. 1740   Cheyennes acquire horses from traders of other
            tribes

1803   United States buys the Louisiana Purchase,
            which includes the Cheyennes' territory

1804   Cheyennes visited by American explorers Meri-
            wether Lewis and William Clark

ca. 1825   Tribe divides into two branches—the Southern
            Cheyenne and the Northern Cheyenne

1851   Cheyennes sign the Treaty of Fort Laramie

1864   Between 400 and 500 Cheyennes are murdered
            by U.S. soldiers at the Sand Creek Massacre

1876   Troops led by General George Custer are killed
            by the Cheyenne warriors during the Battle of Lit-
            tle Bighorn

1877   More than 1,000 Northern Cheyennes join their
            southern kin in present-day Oklahoma

ca. 1887   Many Southern Cheyennes join the Ghost Dance
            Religion

ca. 1900   Tribal land of the Southern Cheyennes is divided
            into allotments owned by individual tribespeople

ca. 1920   Northern Cheyennes' tribal lands are allotted

ca. 1960   Coal discovered on land owned by the Northern
            Cheyennes

GLOSSARY

agent   an employee of the U.S. government charged with conducting official business with an Indian tribe

allotment   U.S. government policy of the late 1800s that sought to divide land owned by a tribe into small tracts owned by individuals; also, one of these tracts

Dog Soldiers   a group of Cheyenne men who were regarded as the tribe's most fierce warriors

Ghost Dance   Indian religion founded in the late 1800s that predicted that whites would disappear from Indian territory and buffalo would return to the Plains

Great Plains   a large area of fairly flat land in the central United States and Canada

massacre   the brutal killing of a group of people who are unable to protect themselves

Quaker   a member of the Society of Friends, a religious group that opposes violence and war

reservation   an area of land set aside for use by Indians

tipi   a portable, cone-shaped house with a wooden frame and covered with animal hides

treaty   a written agreement between two or more groups of people

INDEX

ABOUT THE AUTHOR

Liz Sonneborn is an editor and freelance writer. She lives in New York City.

PICTURE CREDITS